TRAVEL WITH THE GREAT EXPLORERS

Explore with Sir Walter Raleigh

Ruth Daly

Crabtree Publishing Company
www.crabtreebooks.com

Crabtree Publishing Company

www.crabtreebooks.com

Author: Ruth Daly

Managing Editor: Tim Cooke

Designer: Lynne Lennon

Picture Manager: Sophie Mortimer

Design Manager: Keith Davis

Editorial Director: Lindsey Lowe

Children's Publisher: Anne O'Daly

Crabtree Editorial Director: Kathy Middleton

Crabtree Editor: Petrice Custance

Proofreader: Angela Kaelberer

**Production coordinator
and prepress technician:** Tammy McGarr

Print coordinator: Margaret Amy Salter

Written and produced for Crabtree Publishing Company
by Brown Bear Books

Photographs:
Front Cover: istockphoto: tr; **National Gallery of Ireland:** main;
Shutterstock: br, Fedor Selivanov cr.

Interior: **Alamy:** Age Fotostock 20–21b, Art Collection 23t, Chronicle
29b, Granger Historical Picture Archive 16, 17r, Heritage Image
Partnership/Print Collector 19t, Marion Kaplan 25t, North Wind
Picture Archives 13t, 18, 19b, Photos 12/Archives Snark 11c, RooM
the Agency 17tl; **Bridgeman Art Library:** 20; **Dreamstime:** Violet
Paolo 7t, Francisco Rosendo 7b; **Fotolibra:** 13b; **istockphoto:** 6; **Mary
Evans Picture Library:** 10; **National Gallery of Ireland:** 4; **Public
Domain:** Prado 11b; **Shutterstock:** Andrey Eremin 14t, Eric Isselée
22b, Don Mammoser 23b, Maks Narodenko 14bl, Vadim Petrakov
22t; **Thinkstock:** Brian Delft/Dorling Kindersley 12, istockphoto
5bl, 27r, Photos.com 24, 25l; **Topfoto:** 21r, Fine Art Images/HIP 28,
Granger Collection 5r, 5l, 26, 29t, Print Collector/HIP 27bl.
All other artwork and maps, **Brown Bear Books Ltd.**

Brown Bear Books has made every attempt to contact the
copyright holder. If you have any information please contact
licensing@brownbearbooks.co.uk

Library and Archives Canada Cataloguing in Publication

CIP Available at the Library and Archives Canada

Library of Congress Cataloging-in-Publication Data

Names: Daly, Ruth, 1962- author.
Title: Explore with Sir Walter Raleigh / Ruth Daly.
Description: New York, NY : Crabtree Publishing Company, 2018. |
  Series: Travel with the great explorers | Includes index.
Identifiers: LCCN 2017028419 (print) | LCCN 2017030832 (ebook) |
  ISBN 9781427178138 (Electronic HTML) |
  ISBN 9780778739234 (reinforced library binding : alk. paper) |
  ISBN 9780778739388 (pbk. : alk. paper)
Subjects: LCSH: Raleigh, Walter, Sir, 1552?-1618--Juvenile literature. |
  Great Britain--Court and courtiers--Biography--Juvenile literature. |
  Explorers--Great Britain--Biography--Juvenile literature. |
  America--Discovery and exploration--Juvenile literature. |
  Virginia--Discovery and exploration.
Classification: LCC DA86.22.R2 (ebook) | LCC DA86.22.R2 D28 2018 (print) |
  DDC 970.01/7092 [B] --dc23
LC record available at https://lccn.loc.gov/2017028419

Crabtree Publishing Company

www.crabtreebooks.com   1-800-387-7650

Printed in Canada/092017/PB20170719

Published in Canada
Crabtree Publishing
616 Welland Ave.
St. Catharines, ON
L2M 5V6

Published in the United States
Crabtree Publishing
PMB 59051
350 Fifth Avenue, 59th Floor
New York, New York 10118

Published in the United Kingdom
Crabtree Publishing
Maritme House
Basin Road North, Hove
BN41 1WR

Published in Australia
Crabtree Publishing
3 Charles Street
Coburg North
VIC, 3058

CONTENTS

Meet the Boss

Did you know ?

Although the Raleighs were not a noble family, they were prominent in public life. Walter's half-brothers, John, Humphrey, and Adrian Gilbert, and his brother, Carew Raleigh, were advisors to the British court.

Walter Raleigh was born in the west of England in around 1554, but no one is sure of the exact date. He spent his childhood by the sea. Later, he became a favorite of the Tudor ruler, Queen Elizabeth I.

UNKNOWN CHILDHOOD

+ Seafaring father

+ Religious family

Walter Raleigh (right) was the youngest of five sons. His father, also called Walter, was a ship's captain, and the family lived near the coast in Hayes Barton in Devon. Little is known about Raleigh's childhood. He did not go to school but was probably educated at home. As a young man, he studied for a short time at college in Oxford. He then went to fight with the French **Protestants**, or Huguenots, against the Catholics in France in the Wars of Religion (1562–1598).

RALEIGH IN IRELAND

★ A soldier in the English army

★ Receives land as a reward

In his early 20s, Raleigh served as a soldier in Ireland. The Irish, who were mostly Catholic, were rebelling against the rule of the Protestant queen, Elizabeth. Raleigh commanded his own company and fought to put down rebellions against the English. Raleigh gained a reputation for bravery. He also met the queen when he visited the court in London to report on the progress of the military campaign. Raleigh was rewarded for his work with **estates** taken from the Irish rebels.

A FAVORITE

★ **Raleigh meets the queen**

★ **Becomes a knight**

Queen Elizabeth liked Raleigh's outgoing personality and made him one of her **favorites** in 1582. She gave him lands that made him rich, and a knighthood in 1585. But some of the queen's other courtiers disliked him. They were jealous of him and thought he was proud and over-confident.

A SECRET MARRIAGE

☛ **Tragic loss of first child**

In 1591, Raleigh secretly married Elizabeth Throckmorton (right), known as Bess, who was a **lady-in-waiting** to Queen Elizabeth. By then, Raleigh was famous for starting an English **colony** in North America. However, it was illegal for a **courtier** to marry without permission from the queen, and Elizabeth was angry when she found out. Raleigh and Bess had a son the following year, named Damerei, but the baby died from the **plague**.

BANISHED TO THE TOWER!

+ Poet and Prisoner

In June 1592, Elizabeth sent Raleigh and his wife to prison in the Tower of London (left) as punishment for marrying without her consent. Raleigh spent some of his time in prison writing poetry. Raleigh and Bess were released after two months, when one of Raleigh's ships returned to England with treasure from a captured Spanish ship.

Famous Poet

Raleigh wrote poems using simple, direct language. His poems were usually short and about personal matters. His most popular poems included "The Lie" and "A Farewell to False Love."

Where Are We Heading?

Raleigh planned several expeditions to the Americas. The queen kept him at court at first, but he later became the first European to visit Guiana (now Guyana) in South America.

Big River

The Orinoco River stretches from the mountains of Venezuela to the Atlantic Ocean. Its name means "a place to paddle" in the language of the local Warao people.

TO VIRGINIA

☛ Expanding the empire

☛ But you can't go!

In 1584, Queen Elizabeth gave Raleigh permission to explore far-off parts of the world. She wanted to become a more powerful ruler, and she wanted England to rival the **empire** Spain had created in the New World, or the Americas, after Christopher Columbus had sailed there in 1492. Raleigh believed the Americas contained **resources** such as gold. He sent expeditions to establish a colony in North America. He named the land Virginia for Elizabeth, who was known as the Virgin Queen because she never married.

ROANOKE

+ The first settlement

Raleigh chose Roanoke, a sandy island off what is now North Carolina (above), as the site for his settlement. Several European families moved there, but they faced problems including hostile Native peoples, poor harvests, and a lack of supplies. The island was abandoned in 1586, then resettled in 1587. The last group to live there disappeared mysteriously in 1590, and Roanoke became known as the Lost Colony.

> " Whosoever commands the sea commands the trade; whosoever commands the trade of the world commands the riches of the world, and, consequently, the world itself."
> *Walter Raleigh on English attempts to build an empire.*

TRAVEL UPDATE

Follow the River

★ Travelers heading into regions without roads should try using rivers as highways. Raleigh followed the Orinoco River (right), which flows for 1,498 miles (2,410 km) and has many **tributaries** and a broad **delta**. The rivers carried Raleigh and his men through dense rain forests, grassy plains, and mangrove swamps.

FALLS OF THE CARONÍ

☛ Impressive spectacle

As he explored the Orinoco, Raleigh described coming across a dozen waterfalls. He said that each one rose over the other as high as a church tower. He recorded that the water fell with such great fury that it seemed to create a permanent shower of rain in the air. Some people claim that Raleigh had discovered Angel Falls, the highest waterfall in the world. More likely, he had found falls on the Caroní River (left), close to where it meets the Orinoco River.

CITY OF GOLD

★ Promise of riches

★ Pulls Raleigh onward

One of Raleigh's goals in Guiana was to find a legendary city called El Dorado, which Spanish stories claimed was built from gold. Raleigh believed the city was in the mountains at the head of the Caroní River. The story of El Dorado was originally about a native leader who coated himself in gold dust. The story eventually included a city of gold. Raleigh believed that Guiana must have gold mines similar to those used by the Aztec in Mexico and the Inca in Peru.

WALTER RALEIGH'S VENTURES IN THE NEW WORLD

Walter Raleigh did not himself visit the colony at Roanoke in North Carolina, although he came close. But he did make two visits to Guiana, to seek the city of El Dorado in the highlands up the Orinoco River.

NORTH AMERICA

Virginia

In 1584, Raleigh gave the name Virginia to the coast in the North Carolina region. After the failure of the Lost Colony, Virginia became the site of the first permanent English colony, set up at Jamestown in 1607.

Locator map

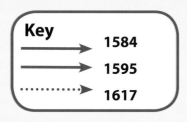

Key

→ 1584

→ 1595

┈┈➤ 1617

Spanish Main

Spain controlled the Spanish Main, the name given to the Caribbean and Atlantic coasts of what are now Mexico and northern South America. Raleigh was eager to weaken Spain's power in the region and replace it with English influence.

Roanoke

Raleigh sent two expeditions to try to establish an English colony on Roanoke, a sandy island off the coast of what is now North Carolina. The first arrived in June 1585, but the settlers returned home the following summer. A second expedition arrived in July 1587. The colony was found abandoned in August 1590. No clue was found about the fate of what became known as the Lost Colony.

● **Sault Sainte Marie**

■ **Jamestown**

VIRGINIA

Roanoke

ENGLAND

Scale ├─── 310 miles ───┤
        └─── 500 km ───┘

Orinoco Delta

The fan-shaped Orinoco Delta covers more than 16,852 square miles (43,646 sq km). Raleigh established good relations with the Warao and Tivitivas people in the region.

Santo Tomé

In January 1618, ships led by Raleigh's lieutenant, Lawrence Kemys, raided this Spanish settlement on the Orinoco River despite orders from King James I not to attack Spanish colonies. The attack had disastrous consequences for Raleigh.

Morequito

Raleigh and his explorers visited this important port near the junction of the Orinoco and Caroní Rivers. They met important local chiefs there, including Topiawari, the king of the region.

El Dorado

In the early 1500s, Spanish explorers began to tell stories about El Dorado, a legendary Native chief covered in gold. Over time, the story had changed to describe a golden city. Raleigh heard the stories. He believed the city stood on a lake named Parime in what is now Venezuela.

Meet the Crew

Walter Raleigh met and worked with different types of people, from rulers and tribal leaders to soldiers and sailors. While he had close friends, many people found him arrogant.

Close Friend

Lawrence Kemys sailed with Raleigh on three voyages to Guiana. In 1618, his men attacked a Spanish settlemen against the orders of King James I. Knowing this would reflect badly on Raleigh, Kemys killed himself.

ELIZABETH I

+ Tudor monarch

+ Keeps Raleigh close to home

Elizabeth was impressed with Raleigh's skills as a soldier in Ireland and was attracted to his **chivalrous** and charming personality. When Raleigh organized his expeditions to found a colony in Virginia, Elizabeth did not allow him to go on the voyage himself. She wanted him to remain with her at court. However, after Raleigh displeased the queen by getting married, he tried to win back her favor by sailing to Guiana to try to claim El Dorado for England. Although he failed, he did manage to make himself popular with the queen again.

FAMOUS POET

★ **Author of *The Fairie Queen***

Raleigh's friend Edmund Spenser was one of the most famous Elizabethan poets. Spenser's main work is a long poem called *The Faerie Queene*. Its characters and scenes were based on historical events and real people of the time. Queen Elizabeth liked the poem so much she rewarded Spenser with a pension for the rest of his life.

Did you know ?

A famous story claimed that once, when Queen Elizabeth I was out walking, she came to a patch of muddy, wet ground. Walter Raleigh laid his cloak on the ground to ensure that she kept her feet dry (above).

HUMPHREY GILBERT

☛ Older half-brother

Raleigh and his half-brother Humphrey Gilbert shared an interest in sailing and exploration. In 1578, they both set out to sail to North America on the same expedition, although they did not reach their destination. Gilbert later returned alone to North America, this time to Newfoundland, where he claimed some fishing settlements for England but did not establish any colonies. He drowned in a shipwreck on the voyage home.

My Explorer Journal

★ Imagine that you are John White. What sort of arguments could Walter Raleigh use to persuade you to give up your comfortable life in England to become the governor of a new colony at Roanoke?

JOHN WHITE

★ Artist and mapmaker

The artist and **cartographer** John White was the first governor of the Roanoke colony. He drew and painted local Algonquin peoples and details of their lives. White illustrated how they fished and farmed, cultural rituals such as dances, and the clothes they wore. He also drew maps of the Virginia coast (left).

A NEW MONARCH

☛ James I dislikes Raleigh

Queen Elizabeth died in 1603, and the English throne passed to King James I. Unlike Elizabeth, James wanted to make peace with Spain. When Raleigh was **framed** for plotting against the king, James locked Raleigh in the Tower of London for **treason**. James allowed Raleigh out to make another attempt to find El Dorado, but when Raleigh failed, he was sent back to prison.

Check Out the Ride

Walter Raleigh's main method of transportation was water. Like other English sailors of the time, he used fast sailing ships. He used smaller boats to explore the Orinoco River.

Big Ship

The *Ark Raleigh* was one of the largest ships of its time. It had four masts and three rows of cannons on each side. However, the ship rolled in heavy seas, making the sailors feel sick!

ONE SHIP, TWO NAMES

+ Raleigh's own ship

In 1586, Walter Raleigh ordered his own **galleon** to be constructed. It was named the *Ark*, but came to be called *Ark Raleigh* (right). At the time, it was a tradition for ships to be named after their owners. In 1587, Queen Elizabeth I bought the ship from Raleigh for use by the Royal Navy. The ship fought in the defeat of the Spanish Armada in 1588, and was later renamed the *Ark Royal*. It served as an English flagship until 1636, when it sank.

TRAVEL UPDATE

Stay Waterproof!

★ Anyone who travels on a wooden ship knows the importance of sealing the planks of the **hull**. If you're near the island of Trinidad, you're in luck! Local Carib people there showed Walter Raleigh a lake of **pitch** when he visited in 1595. Raleigh heated the black tar and spread it over the seams and joints of the ship's deck and hull. When the tar hardened, the seal was waterproof.

★ **Imagine you are one of the explorers in an open boat on the Orinoco. What ways can you think of to pass the long hours traveling on the river?**

THE SEA DOGS

☞ **Acting like pirates**

☞ **On behalf of the Queen!**

The Sea Dogs was the name given to a group of English **privateers**, including Walter Raleigh, Francis Drake, John Hawkins, and Martin Frobisher. They had permission from Elizabeth I to attack the ships of England's enemies, such as Spain. The Sea Dogs used fast, maneuverable ships (above) to attack Spanish ships and colonies. Elizabeth received a share of any treasure they captured. She treated the Sea Dogs as favorites because of the success of their attacks.

Weather Forecast

TROPICAL TIMES

The region of the Orinoco River has a tropical climate. It is warm all the time, though there are wet and dry seasons. Raleigh and his men found it miserable traveling on uncovered boats. The air was humid, and the men were exposed to heavy rainstorms that soaked them to the skin.

OPEN BOATS

★ **River exploration**

★ **No large ships**

The Orinoco River was not deep enough for ships, so Raleigh used a small sailboat called a gallego, two rowboats, a barge, and a ship's boat to travel upstream. The vessels carried a hundred men and their supplies. Local people traveled on the river in canoes hollowed out of logs (left).

Solve It With Science

Raleigh's journeys brought together European technology and the skills of Native peoples in sciences such as astronomy and agriculture.

Stargaze

Raleigh noted that Native peoples used the stars for **navigation**. They gave the constellations names, and told stories about them. Native peoples also used stars to predict the weather.

INTERNATIONAL EXCHANGE

+ **Traveling plants**

+ **Change Europe's diet**

Walter Raleigh's explorations were important in introducing new crops from the Americas to Europe. When the first colonists from Roanoke returned to England, they brought corn, tobacco, and potatoes. The Spanish had already introduced tobacco and potatoes to Europe, but Raleigh helped make them more popular. The potato became an important source of nutrition in European countries such as Ireland, where Raleigh grew potatoes on his estates.

METALWORKER

★ **Expert at Roanoke**

★ **Builds metals laboratory**

One of the first settlers at Roanoke, Joachim Gans, was a **metallurgist** from Bohemia. Gans was experimenting with new ways to extract copper from its rocky ore for making tools and instruments such as compasses. Gans went to Roanoke to search for gold, silver, copper, and iron. He and Thomas Harriot built a laboratory nearby where they could conduct experiments on local minerals.

My Explorer Journal

★ **Using the Internet, choose a star constellation and make up a new story to describe its shape and how it might have been formed.**

> They thought they were rather the works of gods than men."
> *Harriot describes the reaction of Manteo and Wanchese to European inventions.*

SCIENTIST AND LINGUIST

☛ Harriot learns the language

Thomas Harriot was a mathematician and astronomer hired by Raleigh to help with navigation and ship design. Harriot was also a linguist, so when Raleigh brought two Native leaders to London, Manteo and Wanchese, he asked Harriot to work with them. Harriot learned the Algonquian language and created an alphabet. In 1585, Harriot sailed to Roanoke to make maps of the region. He drew various species of plants and animals, and noted Native habits, such as barbecuing food (above left).

CONTRASTING RESPONSES

★ Native reaction varies

While Manteo was friendly toward the English, the warrior Wanchese was more suspicious. The reactions of the two men (left) mirrored the reactions of Native peoples, with some welcoming and some distrusting the newcomers. Whatever the response, the arrival of Europeans would have lasting consequences for Native peoples. Those consequences were nearly all harmful, such as the introduction of deadly European diseases.

Hanging at Home

Raleigh mostly enjoyed a comfortable and privileged life, unless he was traveling in the Americas. Then he fell out of favor with the royal family and their court.

SETTLEMENT

☞ Soldiers and craftsmen

☞ Sent to the New World

Although the first expedition to Roanoke consisted mainly of soldiers, Raleigh also sent **sawyers**, brick makers, and other craftsmen who could help build a settlement (above). The colonists built a star-shaped fort for defense and **thatched** cottages similar to British cottages. These were to be homes for the leaders of the colony. The colonists also built barracks for the soldiers, along with a jail, storehouse, and a workshop for making metal objects.

DURHAM HOUSE

★ A London home

★ At the monarch's pleasure

In 1583, as a reward for his service in Ireland, Queen Elizabeth allowed Raleigh to live in Durham House in London. The home had a courtyard, garden, stables, a large hall, and a chapel. Raleigh had a study in a little turret overlooking the Thames River. When Elizabeth died, King James I ordered Raleigh to leave Durham House.

Raleigh met the Warao people in the Orinoco Delta. They spent half the year living in houses on the ground, but when the river flooded, between May and September each year, they had to move. So they built whole towns on stilts (left) or in trees, with some on higher patches of land. The Warao were not able to do any farming because of the annual floods, so they found food by hunting deer and birds, fishing, and gathering fruit and herbs.

TRAVEL UPDATE

On the River

★ Raleigh recorded that the explorers were often short of food on their voyages up the Orinoco River. They got food by fishing and shooting rainforest birds with their muskets. There was also a variety of edible fruit and plants. These were vital for their survival because they had few supplies.

 **Weather Forecast**

ON THE BOATS

Raleigh complained that the boats on the Orinoco left the explorers exposed to the burning sun and pouring rain. Their clothes were permanently wet, so the men were always uncomfortable. The boats were cramped, the men had to sleep on the hard boards, and they were short of food and clean water to drink.

> " There was never any prison in England that could be found more unsavory and loathsome."
> *Raleigh describes being in uncovered boats on the Orinoco River.*

Meeting and Greeting

The settlers Raleigh sent to Roanoke had both positive and negative encounters with the people they met. Some encounters led to violence.

Baptism

The second group of colonists in Roanoke were led by John White. White's granddaughter, Virginia Dare, was the first English person born in America, in August 1587. She was baptized in Roanoke (below).

THE COLONISTS

- ☛ Settlers needed!
- ☛ Social skills essential

When Raleigh set up the Roanoke colony, he offered any family willing to move there at least 500 acres (202 hectares) of land. In return, the families paid for their own voyage across the Atlantic. Raleigh chose colonists who would be able to govern themselves and trade with local peoples. The colonists also had to have practical skills because they would need to construct and maintain buildings, find and preserve food, and prepare fields for their crops.

THE CROATOAN

- ★ Helpful friends
- ★ Useful information

The Croatoan lived on a narrow island about 50 miles (80 km) south of Roanoke. They lived off the land by farming, hunting, and fishing. Although some Native peoples were hostile toward the colonists, the Croatoan were friendly. The Croatoan helped the colonists in many ways. They gave them food, helped them to understand the politics between the different Native tribes, and showed them the features of the land.

GOOD RELATIONS

★ A friendly welcome

★ Living peacefully

When the first group of colonists arrived in Roanoke, they got on well with local peoples (right). The Native peoples helped show the newcomers where to plant crops and set fishing traps. The settlers could probably have done these tasks themselves, but they were grateful for the help. The two groups lived peacefully together for some time.

Did you know ?

Manteo, the Croatoan chief taken to England in 1584 by men from Raleigh's first expedition, acted as a guide for the colonists when he returned to Roanoke. His companion, Wanchese, was less helpful.

BAD NEIGHBORS

+ Silver cup vanishes

+ Englishman reacts terribly

Some Native groups (left) were suspicious of the Europeans from the start, but a single event turned even friendly Native peoples against the settlers. An English military commander named Richard Grenville discovered that a silver cup was missing from his belongings. He blamed local people, and burned down a Native village in revenge. Native peoples stopped trading with the settlers, who could not get the supplies they needed. When Francis Drake called at Roanoke in 1586, many colonists decided to return with him to England.

More Encounters

Raleigh met different groups of Native peoples in South America. He wrote many accounts of their traditions and stories, and of how the Native peoples lived.

RALEIGH'S MESSAGE

★ Love Queen Elizabeth

★ But don't trust the Spaniards

Raleigh tried to persuade local peoples to show loyalty to England rather than Spain (right). He promised the chiefs that in return for their help in his quest to find gold and El Dorado, the English would protect them from the Spanish. He explained that Elizabeth I was not only a powerful queen but also an enemy of Spain. Raleigh showed them a portrait of the queen. He noted that Native peoples worshiped the image, and named the queen "Elizabeth, the Great Princess, or Greatest Commander."

WATERBORNE

☛ 'Warao' means boat people

☛ Trade with Europeans

In the Orinoco Delta, Raleigh met the Warao people, who were **hunter-gatherers**. The Warao had been driven from their homelands by the Arawak peoples and Dutch explorers. Now they lived in small thatched huts on rivers and in marshlands (right). The Warao had a reputation for being excellent canoeists.

HEADLESS PEOPLE

+ Do the Ewaipanoma exist?

+ Raleigh exaggerates his story

On the Orinoco, Raleigh heard about a people called the Ewaipanoma who had no heads. Instead, they were said to have eyes in their shoulders and mouths in the middle of their chests, while their hair grew between their shoulders (right). Raleigh said he believed the stories were true. In fact, the first account of a headless people called the Blemmyes had appeared in English in the 1300s. Raleigh may have included the story to help make his book of travels more interesting.

Tivitivas

The Tivitivas of the Orinoco Delta had a similar way of life as the Warao. They hunted deer and wild pigs, fished, and used palmetto leaves to make bread. They traded dugout canoes with other tribes for gold and tobacco.

My Explorer Journal

★ Imagine you are a Native chief talking to Walter Raleigh. Make up a description of the strangest type of people you can think of and try to convince the explorer that they really exist.

A LOCAL LEADER

☞ Topiawari is 100 years old

☞ Describes wealthy culture

An elderly chief named Topiawari visited Raleigh at a river port called Morequito. He told Raleigh about local peoples and described a wealthy group living in the mountains. Raleigh assumed this culture must be related to the Incas of Peru and that the city must be the lost city of El Dorado. Raleigh promised to help Topiawari fight the Spanish if the chief would help him find El Dorado, which was also known as Manoa.

I Love Nature

In his travels along the Orinoco River, Raleigh saw animals and plants he had never seen before. He and his crew had to live off the land to survive.

Exaggeration!

Writing about the landscape along the Orinoco, Raleigh said, "I never saw a more beautiful country, nor more lively prospects." Raleigh was probably exaggerating to convince Elizabeth I to send him back to Guiana.

A PERFECT LAND

+ Beautiful paradise

+ Peaceful savannah

Raleigh wrote many descriptions of the beautiful landscape along the Orinoco River. The river passed through rain forest, but it also ran through open **savannah**. Raleigh described seeing wide grassy plains dotted with small clumps of forest. This may have been the region now known as the Gran Sabana in Venezuela (right). There were many wild animals roaming the land. Raleigh could not identify them all, although he did recognize deer. He described the animals grazing along the banks of the river.

UNUSUAL ANIMAL

★ **A strange gift**

★ **Tastes like chicken!**

One of the gifts Chief Topiawari gave Raleigh was an armadillo. The animal's body is covered with a hard shell that Native peoples used to make musical instruments. They also ate armadillo meat, despite some species having a strong, unpleasant smell. In Guiana, Raleigh and his men cooked and ate armadillo. They said it tasted similar to chicken and pork.

Topiawari gave Raleigh a pineapple (left), which the explorer described as the "princess of fruits." Wild pineapples grew over large areas of ground, but their bright yellow fruit was not very pleasant. They were about the same size as an apple, but they were stringy, full of seeds, and tasted sour. Raleigh preferred the pineapples grown by local peoples. These fruit were larger and had a more pleasant taste.

TRAVEL UPDATE

Living off Nature

★ Any explorer can only carry a limited amount of supplies. Walter Raleigh's expeditions had to rely on nature for food. They didn't just catch fish and shoot birds and small animals, but also looked for other sources of food. Raleigh once found thousands of turtle eggs on a sandbar. Eggs are a good source of nutrition.

COLORFUL BIRDLIFE

+ New species

+ And useful food!

Raleigh described seeing crimson, orange, purple, and other brightly colored birds along the Orinoco River. The Europeans did not recognize them—but that did not stop them shooting the birds for food. More than 1,000 species of birds live in the Orinoco, many in the Guiana rain forest. They include birds Raleigh would have seen, such as flamingos, toucans, umbrella birds, scarlet ibis (right), and many types of parrots.

Fortune Hunting

Raleigh's adventurous and risky activities earned him considerable wealth. However, he failed to find the gold he hoped for, which left him at the mercy of the changing moods of England's rulers.

ROYAL SERVICE

+ Becoming Sir Walter

Raleigh became wealthy and was able to live comfortably for most of his life because he was a favorite of Queen Elizabeth I (right). The queen gave him a house in London, a knighthood, and a vast amount of land in Ireland. Raleigh made money by farming and renting out the land. However, relying on royal **patronage** had disadvantages. Raleigh's life became difficult when he fell out of favor with Elizabeth—and especially after she died in 1603. King James I took away many of Raleigh's privileges.

TRAVEL UPDATE

English Presence

★ Any explorer sailing to the New World should consider the best purpose for his or her expedition. Raleigh, for example, was interested in setting up colonies in North America. That would increase international trade. But he also saw how Spain became powerful thanks to the amount of gold it had found in the New World. This inspired Raleigh to concentrate on searching for gold in Guiana, rather than establishing colonies there.

> The common soldier shall here fight for gold, and pay himself, instead of pence, with plates of half-a-foot broad."
> *Raleigh describes the riches he hoped to find in South America.*

HUNTING FOR GOLD

- ☞ Was he foolish?
- ☞ Or ahead of his time?

Along the banks of the Orinoco, Raleigh found rocks that he believed were gold, silver, and other precious stones. He saw gold in Native villages and heard stories of huge gold mines in the mountains. Raleigh collected samples to take back to England, but they were not very valuable. However, Raleigh continued to believe that huge gold reserves existed in the region. He was proven right, but not until the 1900s. Today, both Guyana and Venezuela have large gold-mining industries (right).

LUST FOR GOLD

+ Raleigh's wild ambitions

Raleigh's desire to find gold was driven by the great wealth of the Spanish empire. He had heard stories about the treasure found by Spanish explorers in the Aztec empire in Mexico (left) and the Inca empire in Peru. Raleigh believed he could find just as much gold on behalf of England. In fact, he found very little gold compared to the success of the Spanish **conquistadors**. Raleigh's hopes for his expeditions turned out to be wildly unrealistic.

A BESTSELLER

★ Stories from a new land

★ But no support from the Queen

After his first voyage, Raleigh wrote a book called *The Discoverie of Guiana*. He described the Native tribes he met and their culture, the land and natural resources he found, and his belief that there was much gold to be found. The book was a literary success and made Raleigh famous. However, despite his stories of gold, Elizabeth refused to **sponsor** another expedition to Guiana.

This Isn't What It Said in the Brochure!

Raleigh's expeditions to Roanoke and Guiana both faced disappointments, disasters, and tragedy. Even Raleigh's attempts at piracy went wrong.

Poor piracy!

Sailing home from his first voyage to Guiana, Raleigh attacked Spanish pearl-fishing settlements. The Spaniards fought back, and more than 70 Englishmen died for no gains.

THE LOST COLONY

☛ Colonists disappear

☛ With no explanation

Late in 1587, Governor John White sailed from Roanoke to England for supplies. White was delayed by war in Europe and only returned in August 1590. The colonists could not be found. There were no signs of violence, and the only clues as to what had happened were the word Croatoan, the name of a local Native tribe as well as an island, carved onto a fence (above).

MISSING CITY

★ Seeking El Dorado

★ With little luck

Raleigh was eager to discover El Dorado, the legendary city of gold written about by the Spaniards. He was guided by locals, but even with their help, he failed to find it. Topiawari encouraged Raleigh to return with a large army to find the city—but Raleigh realized that the city itself probably did not exist.

UGLY SERPENTS

+ Crocodile-infested waters

+ Not a good place for a swim!

One of the many dangers the explorers faced on the Orinoco River was crocodiles. The river was home to a species known as the Orinoco crocodile. Once, when the Englishmen stopped to collect supplies, one of Raleigh's servants decided to go swimming. In front of everyone, the man was attacked by a crocodile and eaten. Raleigh called the animals "ugly serpents" and noted that the Native peoples named a river after them, the Lagartos. Today, Orinoco crocodiles (right) still live in the river and are the largest **predator** in South America. However, they are critically endangered.

My Explorer Journal

★ Imagine you were with John White when he returned to Roanoke. What steps might you have taken to try to discover the fate of the Lost Colony? Give reasons for your answer.

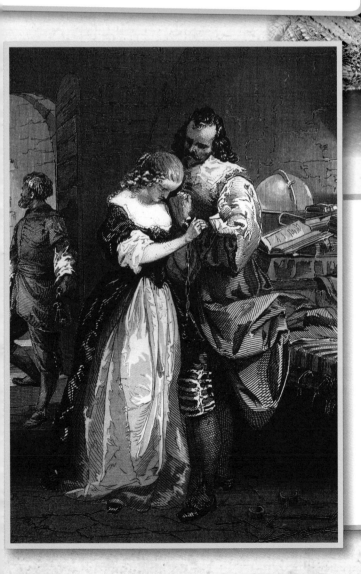

IMPRISONMENT!

★ Framed for plotting

★ Many years in prison

Raleigh was imprisoned in the Tower of London on three occasions. The first time was by Elizabeth I after he married without her consent (left), and the second time was by James I in 1603. Raleigh was framed and falsely accused of plotting against the king. He was held in the Bloody Tower for 16 years. The third time he was imprisoned was after he returned from his second voyage to Guiana.

End of the Road

King James I gave Raleigh one last chance to earn his favor, but Raleigh's final voyage led to disaster. Raleigh's long service to England ended not in glory but in disgrace.

Disaster!

On the way home from Guiana, Raleigh's lieutenant Lawrence Kemys attacked a Spanish outpost against orders. Raleigh's son died in the attack. Raleigh was furious with Kemys, who killed himself.

SECOND VOYAGE

- A chance to make amends
- Father and son sail together

In 1617 James I released Raleigh from his imprisonment in the Tower of London. He gave Raleigh the chance to make a second expedition to Venezuela to search for El Dorado. This time Raleigh was accompanied by his 24-year-old son, Wat (right as a child, with his father). The king specifically ordered Raleigh not to attack any Spanish ships or colonies. James was determined to keep the peace with Spain.

SENTENCED TO DEATH

+ Chooses not to escape

When Raleigh returned to England, he was taken to London and put back in the Tower. The Spanish were angry about the attack on their settlement at Santo Tomé. They persuaded King James to punish Raleigh, even though he had not been involved in the attack. James had not pardoned Raleigh from his previous conviction for treason, so he restored the death sentence. Raleigh had many chances to escape but chose not to. He believed he should take his punishment like a gentleman.

OFF WITH HIS HEAD

+ Final words

Raleigh was executed on October 29, 1618, at the Palace of Westminster in London (right). In the moments before his death, he spoke to the crowd and the executioner. Speaking about being beheaded with an ax, Raleigh said, "This is sharp medicine; but it is a sure cure for all diseases. What dost thou fear? Strike, man, strike." After Raleigh's death, his wife, Bess, kept his **embalmed** head in a velvet bag until she died.

> "It is at this hour my ague [fever] comes upon me. I would not have my enemies think I quaked with fear." *Raleigh tells his executioner to hurry with his execution.*

LASTING REPUTATION

☛ **Success and failure**

☛ **Setting the tone**

Throughout his life, Walter Raleigh fell in and out of favor with royalty. Like other English navigators, he sailed to the Americas (left) but failed to limit the influence of Spain. He also failed in his attempts to establish a colony in the New World and in his search for gold. However, his success in forming good relationships with Native peoples, his knowledge of the various tribes, and his belief that English colonies could be created overseas helped future explorers who sought to expand the British Empire.

GLOSSARY

cartographer Someone who draws maps

chivalrous Polite and well-mannered, especially toward women

colony A settlement controlled by a country in a foreign land

conquistadors Spanish adventurers exploring the "New World" of the Americas

courtier Someone in a royal court who acts as an advisor or companion of the king or queen

delta A fan-shaped area where a river divides into many channels as it meets the sea

embalmed Preserved with chemicals

empire A large territory with a single ruler

estates Extensive properties in the countryside, often used for farming

favorites People whom a monarch treats with special favor and privilege

framed Proved guilty of a crime by the use of false evidence

galleon A large warship powered by sails

hull The main body of a ship or boat

hunter-gatherers People who live by hunting food, fishing, and collecting wild plants and berries rather than farming

lady-in-waiting A woman who helps look after a queen or princess

metallurgist Someone who studies metals and minerals

navigation The skill of figuring out one's location and planning a route

patronage Financial support given to a business or venture

pitch A sticky tarlike substance used for waterproofing

plague A highly contagious disease that is often fatal

predator An animal that preys on others for food

privateers Ship owners given permission by a government or monarch to attack the ships of foreign powers

Protestants People who follow a branch of Christianity that appeared in the 1500s

resources Useful materials from the natural world

savannah Grassy plains with few trees

sawyers People who saw timber as a job

sponsor To pay for something

thatched Roofed with dry grass and straw

treason The crime of betraying one's country

tributaries Rivers that flow into a larger river

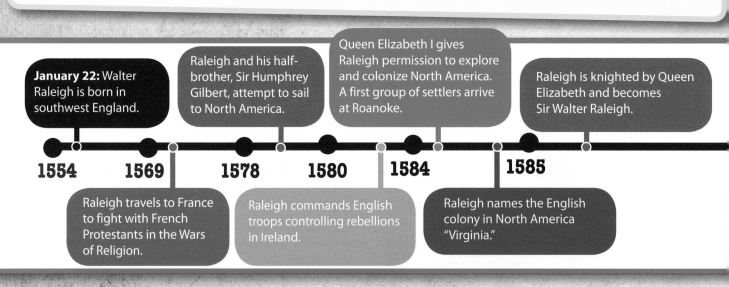

January 22: Walter Raleigh is born in southwest England.

Raleigh and his half-brother, Sir Humphrey Gilbert, attempt to sail to North America.

Queen Elizabeth I gives Raleigh permission to explore and colonize North America. A first group of settlers arrive at Roanoke.

Raleigh is knighted by Queen Elizabeth and becomes Sir Walter Raleigh.

1554   **1569**   **1578**   **1580**   **1584**   **1585**

Raleigh travels to France to fight with French Protestants in the Wars of Religion.

Raleigh commands English troops controlling rebellions in Ireland.

Raleigh names the English colony in North America "Virginia."

ON THE WEB

www.rmg.co.uk/discover/explore/sir-walter-raleigh?gclid=CNaMllzIg9QCFe4y0wods7clsw
A page about Walter Raleigh's life and achievements from the Royal Museum at Greenwich, London.

primaryfacts.com/3040/sir-walter-raleigh-facts-and-information/
A fact sheet about Walter Raleigh's life for children.

www.bbc.co.uk/education/clips/zyf7xnb
A video about young explorers today recreating the voyages of Sir Walter Raleigh.

www.ducksters.com/history/colonial_america/lost_colony_of_roanoke.php
A Ducksters' page about the Lost Colony of Roanoke.

www.softschools.com/timelines/sir_walter_raleigh_timeline/149/
A timeline of Walter Raleigh's life.

BOOKS

Holler, Sherman (ed.). *Biographies of Colonial America: Raleigh, Powatan, Phyllis Wheatley* (Impact on America: Collective Biographies). Rosen Publishing Group, 2012.

Levy, Janey. *Roanoke: The Lost Colony* (History's Mysteries). Gareth Stevens Publishing, 2015.

Petrie, Kristin. *Sir Walter Raleigh* (Explorers). Checkerboard Library, 2007.

Schuetz, Kari. *Roanoke: The Lost Colony* (Abandoned Places). Bellwether Media, 2017.

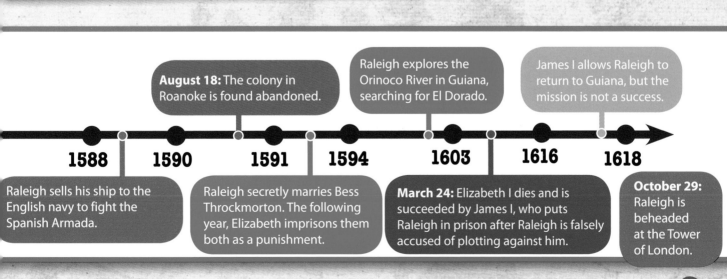

August 18: The colony in Roanoke is found abandoned.

Raleigh explores the Orinoco River in Guiana, searching for El Dorado.

James I allows Raleigh to return to Guiana, but the mission is not a success.

1588   **1590**   **1591**   **1594**   **1603**   **1616**   **1618**

Raleigh sells his ship to the English navy to fight the Spanish Armada.

Raleigh secretly marries Bess Throckmorton. The following year, Elizabeth imprisons them both as a punishment.

March 24: Elizabeth I dies and is succeeded by James I, who puts Raleigh in prison after Raleigh is falsely accused of plotting against him.

October 29: Raleigh is beheaded at the Tower of London.

INDEX